FIDDLER ON THE ROOF

Solo Violin with Piano Reduction

Music by JERRY BOCK
Words by SHELDON HARNICK

Adaptation, arrangement,
and violin cadenzas by
JOHN WILLIAMS

ISBN 978-1-4234-1018-8

Visit Hal Leonard Online at
www.halleonard.com

HAL•LEONARD®
CORPORATION
7777 W. BLUEMOUND RD. P.O. BOX 13819 MILWAUKEE, WI 53213

From its inception, Jerry Bock and Sheldon Harnick's "Fiddler on the Roof" has been recognized as a masterpiece in the annals of American musical theater.

When in the early 1970s the United Artists Corporation decided to film the musical, they wisely chose the young and extremely talented Norman Jewison to be the movie's director, and he in turn invited me to join him as his music director for the project. For what was one of the happiest years of my life, I served as pianist, choral arranger, orchestrator and conductor, working alongside Mr. Jewison as he realized his magnificent film.

In the process of developing the movie, it was clear that it would need additional music not provided in the theatrical production. The opening of the film was a case in point. The establishing scenes and opening credits needed an extended musical accompaniment, so I decided to write an original cadenza and a set of decorative variations based on Jerry Bock's themes that would serve as an overture to the film.

Our soloist on the soundtrack recording was the immortal Isaac Stern, in whose memory I lovingly dedicate this piece. Whatever pleasure violinists and listeners may derive from this music will be a source of joy for me, and will further memorialize Jerry Bock and Sheldon Harnick's great achievement.

John Williams

FIDDLER ON THE ROOF

Music by JERRY BOCK
Words by SHELDON HARNICK

Adaptation, arrangement,
and violin cadenzas by
JOHN WILLIAMS